I0794218

BROKEN RECORDS

ACCIDENTAL RECORDS
TO MAKE YOU GO OOPS!

KENNY ABDO

Fly!
An Imprint of Abdo Zoom
abdobooks.com

abdobooks.com

Published by Abdo Zoom, a division of ABDO, P.O. Box 398166, Minneapolis, Minnesota 55439. Copyright © 2024 by Abdo Consulting Group, Inc. International copyrights reserved in all countries. No part of this book may be reproduced in any form without written permission from the publisher. Fly!™ is a trademark and logo of Abdo Zoom.

Printed in the United States of America, North Mankato, Minnesota.
052023
092023

THIS BOOK CONTAINS RECYCLED MATERIALS

Photo Credits: Alamy, AP Images, Everett Collection, Getty Images, Shutterstock, ©Fred Syversen p15
Production Contributors: Kenny Abdo, Jennie Forsberg, Grace Hansen
Design Contributors: Candice Keimig, Neil Klinepier, Laura Graphenteen

Library of Congress Control Number: 2022946933

Publisher's Cataloging-in-Publication Data

Names: Abdo, Kenny, author.
Title: Accidental records to make you go oops! / by Kenny Abdo
Description: Minneapolis, Minnesota : Abdo Zoom, 2024 | Series: Broken records | Includes online resources and index.
Identifiers: ISBN 9781098281359 (lib. bdg.) | ISBN 9781098282059 (ebook) | ISBN 9781098282400 (Read-to-me ebook)
Subjects: LCSH: Records--Juvenile literature. | History--Juvenile literature. | Accidents--Juvenile literature.
Classification: DDC 032.02--dc23

TABLE OF CONTENTS

ACCIDENTAL RECORDS

Most people work really hard to break world records. But sometimes, records just happen without people even trying!

Whether they were trying to set a completely different record or just living their lives, some people accidentally claimed a prize that no one else had!

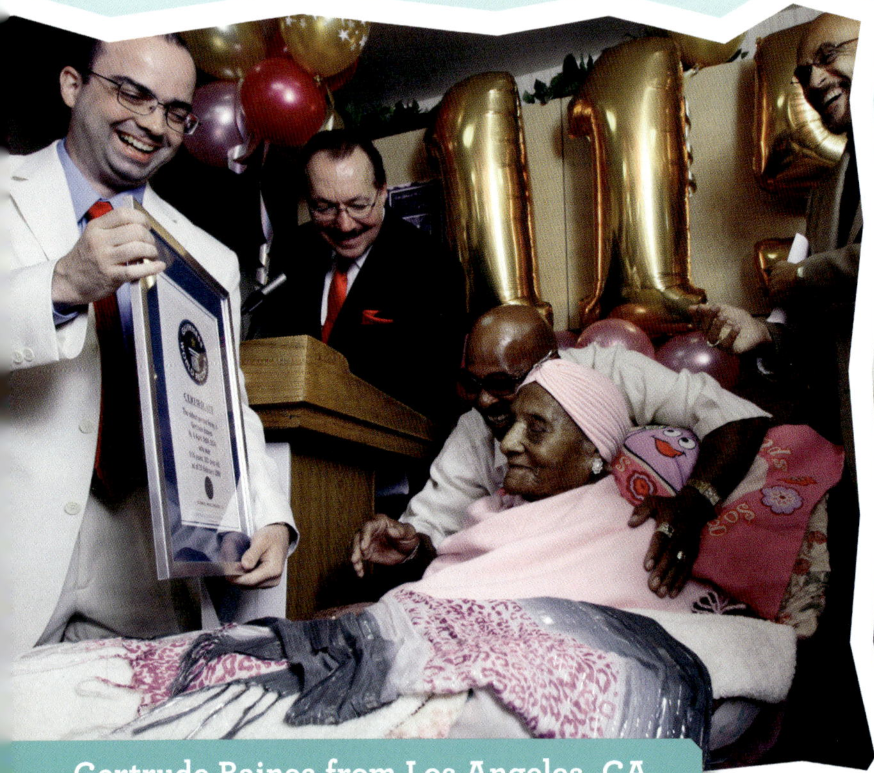

Gertrude Baines from Los Angeles, CA celebrates her 115th birthday in 2009.

WORLD
RECORD
ABBOTT
WORLD
MARATHON
MAJORS

BROKEN RECORDS

Daredevil Evel Knievel was famous for his death defying stunts. By the end of 1975, he had broken his bones 433 times. This was a record no one has wanted to break since!

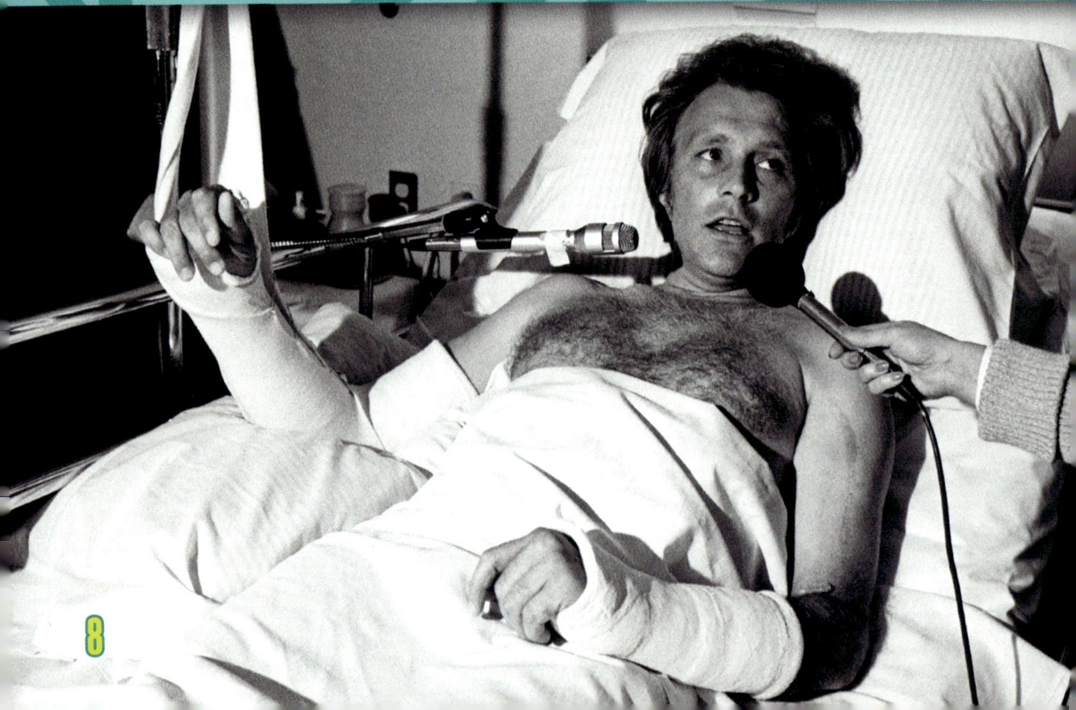

In 2001, Matthew McKnight was hit by a car traveling 70 mph (112.7 kph). He flew 118 feet (36 m). McKnight survived, claiming the world record for farthest auto accident flight survived.

The 2006 James Bond film *Casino Royale* won the **Guinness World Record** for the most **barrel rolls** in a car.

In the scene, 007's **iconic** Aston Martin DBS rolled seven times with stunt driver Adam Kirley at the wheel!

Norwegian skier Fred Syversen **veered** off course in the French Alps and went off a much larger cliff than he'd planned. Syversen unintentionally set a new record for biggest sky cliff jump at 352 feet (107 m). And luckily, he landed safely!

In 2013, an international team of scientists broke a record while making **graphene**. While examining the graphene, the scientists discovered a sheet of glass measuring just two **atoms** thick! It is the thinnest piece of glass known to man.

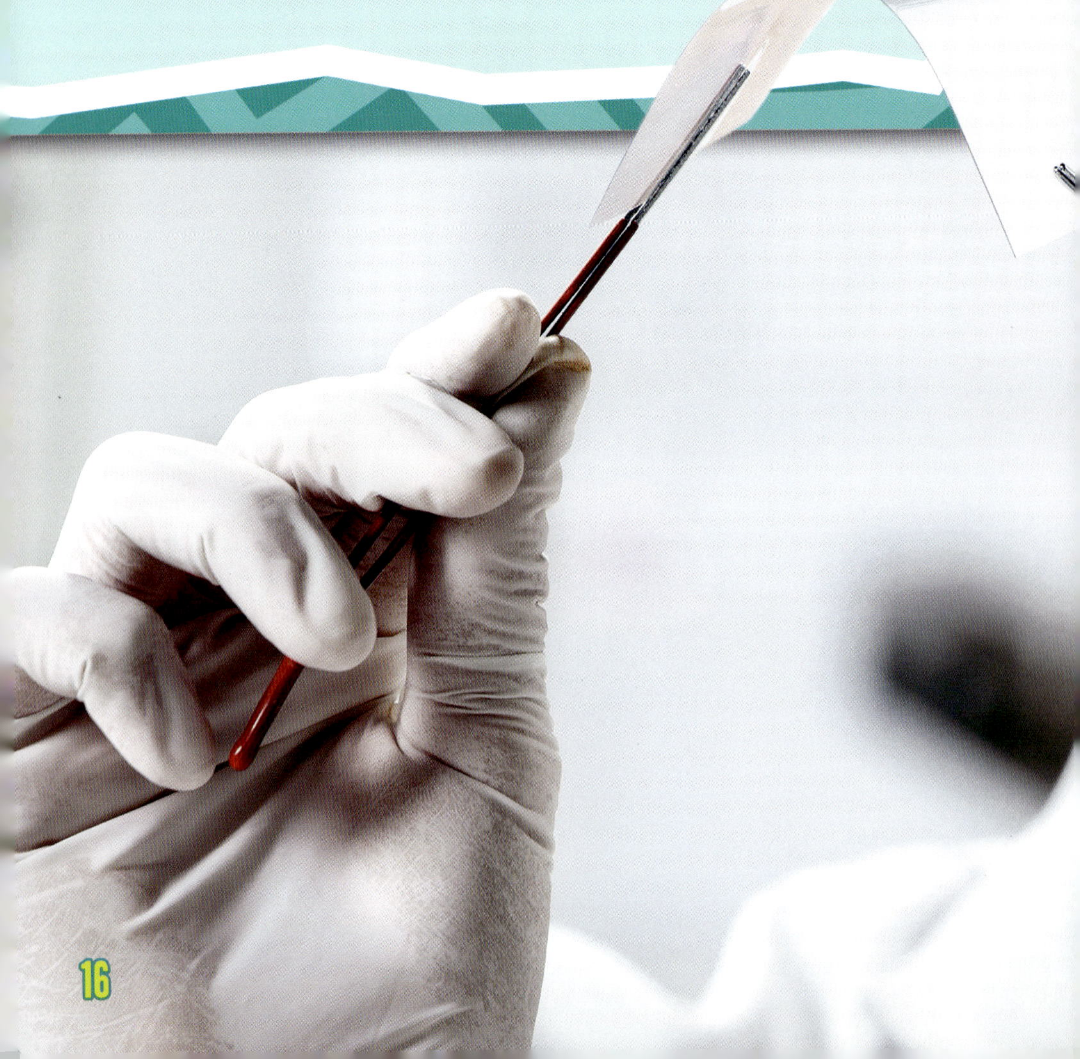

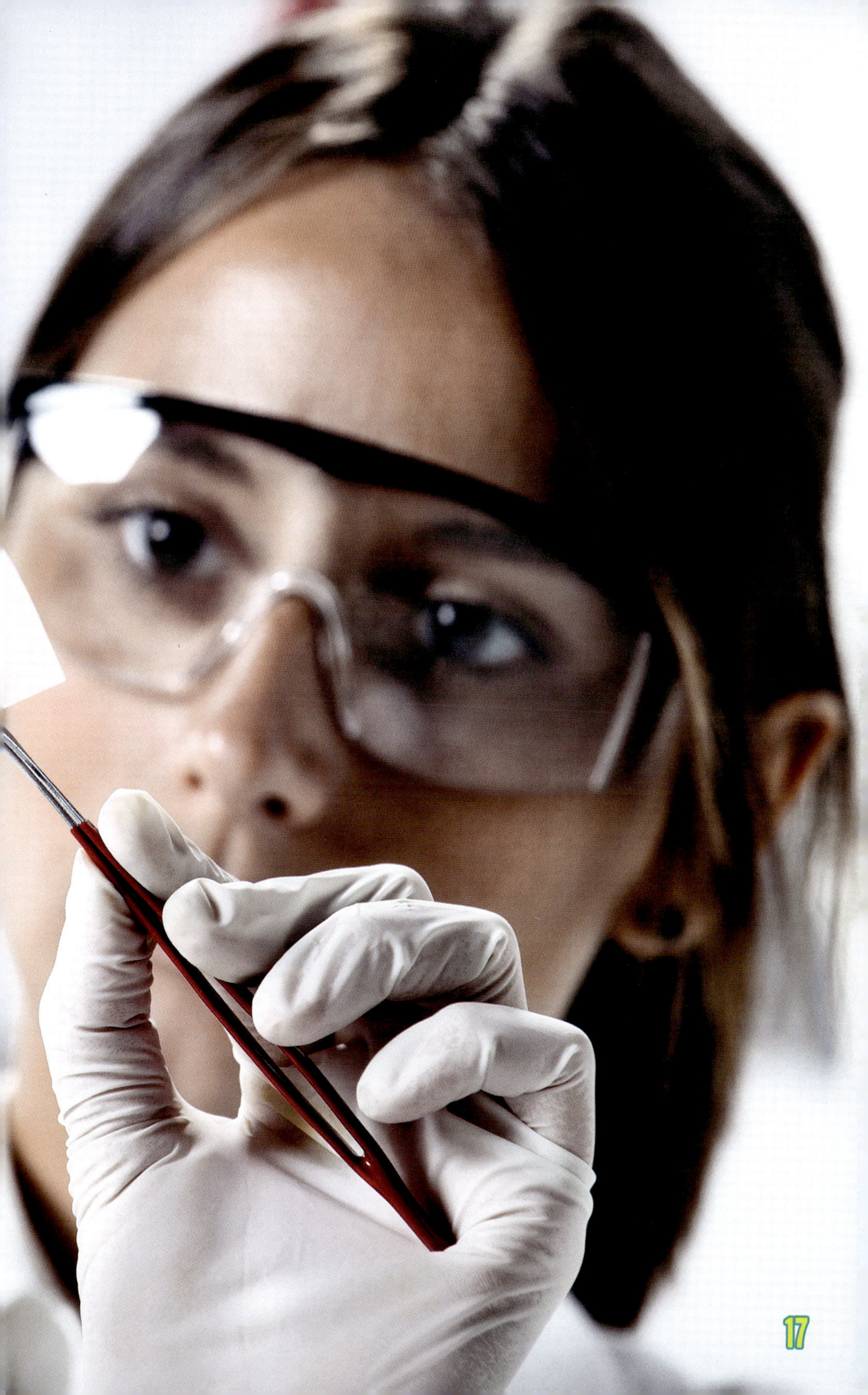

In 2015, swimmer Katie Ledecky broke her own world record in the women's 1500 meter **freestyle** event. Ledecky's time of 15:27.71 seconds beat her former world record by .65 seconds! Even Ledecky was surprised! "It's probably one of the coolest world records I've broken," Ledecky said.

FOR THE RECORD

Even if these incredible achievements happened accidentally, it is always better to break records than to break bones!

GLOSSARY

atom – the smallest possible unit of a chemical element.

barrel roll – a usually accidental occurrence in which a vehicle rolls completely over along its longitudinal axis.

daredevil – a person who performs dangerous and reckless stunts for entertainment.

freestyle – a competitive swimming event in which the swimmers can use any stroke.

graphene – a two-dimensional allotrope of carbon composed of a single layer of carbon atoms arranged in a hexagonal lattice structure. It is very thin but extremely strong.

Guinness World Record – an award given to those who have broken a record never achieved before.

iconic – widely recognizable and well-established by the public.

veer – a sudden change in direction.

ONLINE RESOURCES

Booklinks
NONFICTION NETWORK
FREE! ONLINE NONFICTION RESOURCES

To learn more about accidental records, please visit abdobooklinks.com or scan this QR code. These links are routinely monitored and updated to provide the most current information available.

INDEX